"I dedicate this little window of mine to all those who have supported and endured me over the years, through gestures of empathy, concreteness and affection."

Table of Contents

0. Synopsis

This is a starting point for dealing with different situations and areas.

This is a small guide for those who want to get inspiration on how to best use their skills for functional yet creative writing.

But that's not all it is, it is also a lightweight reading material to the more advanced ones who may want to consider copywriting from a different viewpoint.

Because in an ever-evolving world, mutated and shaped by Internet, which has entered in our lifestyle, our writing also undergoes fundamental changes.

1. Foreword

Social Media have been an integral part of our lives for years now. We use them for leisure activities, for communication purposes, for keeping up to date with world events and much more.

But what does it really mean to be able to speak in a digital world? What does it mean to provide a presence and to build a social channel within a company?

This small manual-guide attempts to answer this point. Because these technological media platforms are constantly evolving, we need to be aware of both the human and relational aspects involved in digital communication.

This must be complemented by a technical knowledge relating to digital tools specific to digital environments. The presentation of subjects we are going to discuss will be of help here: from the more 'obvious' notions to the ones that are not so common and are more inherent to technological solutions on which these social networks are founded.

This little handbook also takes into consideration a significant issue. Nowadays, Social Media is evolving and differentiating very quickly. It is very difficult to give a standardised guidance covering as many situations as possible.

For that reason, all elements covered will focus on a comprehensive and flexible perspective, in order to be more responsive to diverse frameworks and situations, while keeping in mind the more common features found in today's many digital ecosystems.

The goal is to offer the foundations for a proper mindset when approaching writing both in a digital and in a social media context.

2. Social Media Today

Many, different, for all tastes and preferences. Nowadays, social networks follow two distinctive paths.

On one side, Facebook, Instagram and Whatsapp are all trying to retain their audiences by widening their features, in order to become a mainstream platform.

On the other side we find niche contexts which often appeal to a very precise group of people, depending on both common preferences and ages.

Average age is one of the key factors of these years.

Indeed, we are witnessing a stratification - across the board - of age ranges, depending on the nature of the different social networks.

This bears testimony to the concept of social networks as a 'community' of people, which need an environment in which to interact and exchange ideas, items and beliefs with peers. This happens also in the real world, through groups or subcultures.

A similar reasoning can be made in all real world situations, such as when one finds oneself in a public square. In such surroundings, it would be possible to have conversations and witness other people talk.

2.1 A place for communication

If social media are both a medium and a space for conveying ideas, notions and content, why are there different ones?

It comes from a combination between our needs to connect and our surroundings.

Just like in real life, communication is not a one way process and successful interaction also takes advantage of an appropriate context to be more effective.

This is why Instagram is so different from YouTube, which is so different from Linkedin, and so on. These are all eco-systems which already have in their structure a very specific purpose of usage, addressed to certain demands (promoting one's curriculum vitae or showing one's travels, for example).

Once sharing has begun, users can start to respond.

Unlike traditional media such as radio and television, contents shared can be in turn be discussed, commented on, shared again in real time and thus become part of a virtual buzz.

This is how some items become viral, in other words, they achieve such notoriety that they turn into a trend.

We often also speak of Memes, which are contents so appreciated by a certain subculture or a wider audience, that they acquire a remarkable spreading and popularity in a comparatively very short span of time.

Sebbene i social media rivestano tutt'oggi un forte fine ludico e di intrattenimento, sempre di più è presente una finalità di business all'interno degli utilizzi di questi ambienti.

Indeed, social networks are not only populated by individuals or groups, but also by companies, enterprises, institutions and associations which make this environment even more diverse and energetic.

2.2 To be a brand on social media

For quite some time big, medium and even very small companies have been using social media.

There are many reasons for this. A Social Media platform can give a brand a positive boost to its image or heighten public knowledge of its very existence or values and principles.

All with benefits in business activities.

In addition, it is also possible to advertise one's product/service in an immediate manner and calibrate strategy in accordance with tools which measure precise numbers.

Not to be neglected are the possibilities of interacting with the audience. A Brand can interact with all its stackholders via social media.

Stakeholders are what are all those who may have a contribution, even if minimal, in the life of the brand itself (employees, shareholders, colleagues, suppliers, etc.).

A definition that not only covers customers, but also all those who can have even a minimal impact on a brand's life (employees, shareholders, colleagues, suppliers, and so on).

Responding to concerns and enquiries from those who interface directly with your brand is a foundation for a " Social Media Public Relation ", which may have a positive return in terms of renown and appreciation.

Joining a social media context also enables you to respond quickly to the many opportunities offered by the platforms themselves. New ways of distributing content and services are always at the forefront of technological developments in these settings.

In some cases, a social media channel also enables a rapid response to so-called 'communication crises', which are situations where a brand's reputation may be affected by a particular issue.

Such 'crises' have always been a delicate matter, to be treated with utmost sensitivity and social media may not always be the preferable option, but it can be useful when the context determines a need to answer to one' s audience in an instant, synthetic and clear manner.

3. The Copy, this stranger

On Social Media we use image, video, sound but above all texts to convey our messages.

The written word is today still the prevailing medium for building imagery and significance in order to tell and narrate.

This is the context in which copy comes into play. What is a copy?

A copy is a persuasive piece of writing that acquires meaning and purpose depending on the context/environment in which it finds itself and the recipients to which it is addressed.

An example of an ideal explanation of this definition is an analogy to the real world.

We often, for instance, focus on the choice of words we use in a discussion and we also try to organise our lexicon and speech patterns around the existence of particular people and situations so that we speak with greater effectiveness to achieve a specific outcome or result.

Writing a copy is about choosing the right words, style and tone to achieve your desired outcomes.

This is simple from the outside, but complex in its recipe, which not only takes into account creative, but psychological and often more technical criteria.

To acquire skills in Copywriting does not only mean to be able to write 'pleasing' texts, but also to think strategically and in a timely way which aspects of the narration, potential reaction of the target audience and the narrator's identity, should be prioritised in order to achieve the goals that have been considered.

3.1 Social Media Copywriting

A copy, when included in a content from a social channel owned by a brand, can have various purposes including:

- talking about the brand's values, ideas and beliefs

- promoting a product/service

- telling a story about the people and history behind a company, in such a way as to exert empathy with the audience

- telling about the projects and initiatives that put the company in a favourable light and attract the attention of an audience

- providing education. Some companies may use proven expertise or renown in a particular field or business to convey focused and tailored news media content to their audience.

- interface directly with the public. This is often done through surveys, quizzes and the like, which increase the range of interactions available.

- construction/transformation and definition of the perceived image (cause and consequence of the points mentioned above)At this juncture, writing becomes a "bridge" between the needs of the narrator and the desires or curiosities of the readers.

The latter are not only passive "receivers" of the contents, but can themselves contribute to the construction of the meaning, by sharing or questioning the object (whether positive or negative).
In fact, the brand establishes a relationship that is expressed through the tone of voice adopted by the copywriter.

3.2 Tone of Voice

We refer to 'tone of voice' as a particular form of expression in brand Communication.

We distinguish one individual from another by the way they convey who they are in relation to someone else.

So a corporation also mimics this phenomenon in its communications. For instance, two well-known smartphone manufacturers will not use the exact same lexicon, storytelling and contents on their own social networks.

This is either to dilute their own public perception, or to stand out more from their competitors by searching for more identifiable recognition.

The quest for tone-of-voice, through the use of copywriting, can help shape the characteristics that we would like to have perceived by the reader (authoritativeness, freshness, reliability, etc.).

An expositional strategy should not be too "rigid" but rather adaptable to the environment in which the brand operates.

Therefore, it is possible to manipulate the wording so that it can also be adapted to the required protocol in a particular situation.

3.3 How to write

In order to write an effective copy regarding social media content, some basic steps may be followed.

Clarity

Sentences that are not too complex or technical. This allows you to reach a higher proportion of your audience and be more understandable.

Simplicity

The narration should be as smooth as possible. Short sentences with minimal use of any coordinates or subordinates. The benefit is increased readability, notably where there is little space dedicated to writing.

Inclusivity

Unless the text is by necessity aimed at a very targeted and selected audience, it is advisable not to use terms that categorise the final recipient of the message too exclusively. This is in order not to reduce the reaching of your message to your audience. Instead, it is better to omit these types of words and let your text target the reader implicitly, without any connotation.

The role of the story teller

When writing, it is also necessary to consider who the narrator is and how he or she should be positioned within the text.

This is because a brand that presides over a social media channel is considered the 'narrator' by readers.

In the case of brands as companies, it is advisable to use the first person plural.

To express through 'we' when the narration refers to the brand itself, humanizes it and makes the main constituent elements within it visible; people.

Examples:

1. "Brand X is happy to present the new sustainability roadmap for 2025"

2. "We at Brand X are happy to present the new sustainability roadmap for 2025" 3.

3. "We are happy to present the new sustainability roadmap for 2025".

Examples 2 and 3 are more recommended and - in particular - 2 is recommended mainly for very formal and celebratory occasions.

Using narration in this way also works when you want to promote the work of people working for your brand.

Example:

John Doe - our IT manager - is among those who actively contribute to our digitalization journey. The new Moebius project, implemented with his team, will allow us to offer a customer experience that is even closer to our quality objectives.

In this sense, through terms such as "we", "our", the narrator is no longer seen as an abstract entity, but rather as an expression of the company., "we have" "we are" the narrator is no longer seen as an abstract entity, but as a group, more or less large, made up of real people who with their commitment build every day the history, the present and the future of that company.

There are also cases in which the business brand explicitly refers to a personality. One such case is celebrity chefs, who tailor their brand image around their own person.

In these instances, the 'we' rule may be dropped, and instead used when necessity dictates. Thus, for example, when a personality is involved in collaborations, partnerships or needs to promote the collective efforts of his or her team.

3.4 How much to write

Often people ask themselves what is the right amount of characters to use when writing a post.

The response is actually not so straightforward.

While there are boundaries, it is not always advisable to come close to them, but at the same time the opposite can be true. Is the middle ground the solution then? Not really

A perfect copy objectively speaking, would be one from which you do not have to remove or add anything, whilst not losing effectiveness. A definition that is still very ambiguous.

It is precisely because there is no standard for " perfect writing" that there is no quantifiably precise template leading to an " ideal" copy size.

We can however use some general principles.

Smartphones

About 80% of social networks are used from mobile devices. Many smartphones usually do not display very long texts on their screens.

Reading speed

Text is read very quickly on social networks, while the attention span in mainstream environments also tends to be very short. Thus, you should often set out the core ideas of your post within the opening lines (around 155 characters) of your message.

Inclusion of text in other elements

Photos and videos can sometimes help to shorten copy. Copy can be creatively inserted into content and work together along the traditional post hook to make a message more effective.

Emotive appeal of a message

Message length can also be adjusted to obtain a specific reaction in the reader.

A very short copy, less than 155 characters, but incisive can represent a strong brand positioning tool, in relation to certain themes.

A long copy, longer than 600 characters, can instead be used for a highly emotional storytelling, which strikes the heart of the reader.

The same reasoning can be applied to "celebrate" and emphasise a particular achievement, leveraging on common efforts and commitment.

Upper character limits

In each social environment there is a hard cap on characters. It may be more stringent in some platforms, or so high in other environments that it is insignificant.

Based on these considerations, it is always advisable, before proceeding to draft a copy of a length suitable for the intended purpose, to:

- Use publication tools specific to social channels in order to assess and calibrate readability and usability in a mobile environment.

- Consider length of text in relation to communication purposes (promotion, storytelling, information).

- Condense core messages according to standards of clarity, conciseness and simplicity.

4. Not just copy

Copy is not alone. Or rather, copy is not an end in itself but 'dialogues' with other elements within published content or within any interface in which it is inserted.

Indeed, a traditional post can also include text in its graphics as already discussed in 3.4 and some additional components according to which social channel is being considered.

Emojis

Ideograms that can be used as an aid in your copy. They enhance all the significance of a message and can give a lighter and more informal tone to storytelling.

Status

A short complement that denotes a mood or a thought belonging to the storyteller.

Hashtag

A keyword preceded by the '#' symbol. Originally conceived to categorize subjects dealt within a post and to facilitate research by readers, nowadays hashtags take on an identity value in certain contexts, a vector for ideals, principles and values or a 'slogan'. Its use, both in quantitative and in qualitative sense, varies according to social network.

Mention

A nickname preceded by the '@' symbol. Its purpose is to interactively refer to another entity present on that same social network. This may direct your audience towards that entity.

Geotag

An expression denoting where content was created. It can be manually generated and customised on some platforms. Also in some instances, it can assist in the creative expression of a content message, as well as in localised social media marketing initiatives.

Hyperlink

Commonly known as a 'link'. A string that links to another form of digital content. Given their bulk in copy, they are often shortened by functions provided by platform or third-party tools. Text links referring to a web page can also be omitted in favour of thumbnails.

Thumbnail

An interactive box linking to a web page and comprising a title, a description and a presentation image.

This is an element usually reconstructed by a so-called 'crawler', a software entity that takes title, image and description attributes from a website and then reconstructs them as thumbnail posts.

In order for a thumbnail to be reliably and correctly reconstructed, the following Open Graph meta tags should at least be declared in a web page's HTML code under the <head> section:

og:title

og:description

og:image

Without these, the crawler will try to reconstruct the thumbnail less reliably by using other references such as an image on the web page, the meta description and the SEO title tag.

4.1 Call to action principle

Call to action is an explicit invitation to a reader, created and included in a copy, so that the addressee performs a specific action.

CTAs are available in various types. Here are some examples:

- "Click here"
- "Find out more"
- "Sign up for our newsletter"
- "Follow us"
- "Swipe up"

Some symbols or emoji can synthesise and replace certain CTAs such as directional arrows, mail icon, telephone icon, etc..

CTAs should not be as repetitive as possible. Indeed, their strength that is their immediacy is counterbalanced by that of growing old and becoming cloying to readers very quickly.

This is why a diversified and creative use of these functions is advisable.

4.2 Microcopy world

Digital and social media environments are populated by texts that are often very short, sometimes very brief indeed.

Just think about navigation items belonging to a website menu, an email subject line or an Instagram landing page bio.

Call-to-actions discussed in 4.1 can also be considered microcopy expressions.

Most of these extremely short texts are often, due to the need for clarity, extremely 'dry' and direct, in order to be immediately recognisable in their function and meaning.

This doesn't necessarily mean sacrificing creativity, but rather making it a virtuous case of "less is more". This is what happens with many sponsored contents, namely elements that constitute part of an advertising circuit within a social platform.

In this case, a creatively created microcopy containing fewer than about 6 words becomes very effective and attractive as a presentation 'hook' as far as the content itself is concerned (if that is also creatively and strategically studied).

So the outcome as a whole becomes a stimulating experience and discovery for the audience, who are not merely 'subjected' to the interaction, but rather 'attracted' to it.

We are also thinking about elements such as polls, quizzes and stories, which are increasingly popular with the public.

These latter elements have been designed to encourage a more interesting, varied and less 'passive' interaction with readers. It is precisely they who are invited to explore this type of media content.

This is why, here too, 'personalisation' and creativity in displaying messages made up of single or few words becomes an opportunity to make a message more experiential.

Therefore, communication can also take on a 'playful' note that 'plays' with metaphores, symbolism and icons, which fits in well with one of the main reasons why people use social media: entertainment.

However, this does not mean that a more 'sophisticated' or 'hermetic' style of communication is necessarily more rewarded than a more straightforward way of expression.

There must be a skilful use and a deep knowledge of both the host platform and the audience.

It is precisely at this juncture that perhaps the most 'human' side of any consideration given to a 'social' communication strategy comes into play: readers themselves.

5. Readers

Until now, we have always tried to consider our message's recipient when building our copy.

This is not a minor concern. Although the name "addressee" often seems to be perceived with a connotation more akin to "final" or " ultimate", in reality it is indeed the reader himself who should be the starting point on which the formulation of an effective strategy must revolve.

"Knowing your audience' therefore becomes a mantra to bear in mind amongst the best copywriting practices.

Having analysis tools at our disposal, sometimes even supplied natively by the hosting platform, can enable us to know more than just attributes such as age, gender or membership in a particular culture or subculture,

We can also trace, from the data provided, lifestyle, habits or preferences from our readers.

That helps us to tailor our texts as closely as possible to collective trends manifested by our target audience.

The word thus becomes a 'dress' that is 'sewn' around a reader, and message effectiveness is increased, particularly if it is accurately targeted.

Being aware of who is also reading what we are writing enables a greater speed in both the execution and the construction phases of a copy proposal. The copywriter's mind will already be able to discard all those ideas considered "off target" or in any case very far from the desiderata and/or preferences expressed by readers.

Keeping in mind who our "average reader" might be should not only be a sporadic operation in its frequency.

People change over time, as do their interests, habits and the very way they interact with content on social media.

Consequently, attention to the 'morphology' with which the audience is viewed must be constant, whenever one has to think about creating content that brings interaction with viewers.

5.1 A matter of sensibility

In **3.1** we defined copy as also a way of establishing a relationship with our readers.

Just like relations between people, it is necessary to take into account a notion that is also of primary importance: sensibility.

Indeed, the act of reading a piece of social media content, like other experiences, is a component that enters into the experience of its receiver, affecting him or her both emotionally and psychologically.

We must take into account, especially, what consequences our words have towards our intended audience.

For this reason, it is necessary to take into consideration, besides 'knowing one's readers', also to respect their sensibilities, by acting with sensibility.

What does this mean? Knowing how to position yourself. Knowing what reputation on average your readership attributes to a narrator and calibrating your messages accordingly.

Another point is to adhere, also as a storyteller, to netiquette. This is a set of rules preventing the establishment of a 'toxic' environment that is detrimental to healthy interactions with and between readers.

For this reason, it is always advisable to keep a reassuring tone of voice, but above all a human one.

Furthermore, those who are respectful of netiquette should always be considered worthy of respect and consideration. It is advisable not to use provocative tones in your texts or in any case generate an unpleasant feeling of 'inadequacy'. The effects may vary: from the mildest 'cringe', that is a direction that induces precisely a perceived inadequacy in relation to the context, to outright offence. The latter can in turn generate a cascade of damage in the relationship with one's audience.

Good sensibility is also based on having a finger on pulse regarding the so-called 'sentiment', in other words the way a brand's actions are perceived by our target community.

This can be perceived, for instance, through analyzing comments, mail messages, and messaging communications filed by users, who may not be "loyal" subjects or regular visitors to our social environment.

6. Conclusions

We have come to a conclusion, which is however the beginning.

What I would urge you to do is to take on board the concepts expressed so far, and perhaps try to see the posts you happen to see on a daily basis from a different perspective.

Each one has a different approach, a path, a psychological journey that will have led that copywriter to evaluate that mix of ingredients as the most suitable to achieve the given aim.

The most recommended advice, on the other hand, is to always use a comprehensive approach, that is to say, not to see copy as a self-sufficient item but integrated and in osmosis with a multitude of different elements that are influenced by it, but that can also influence it.

All that has been presented can be seen as a starting kit on the trip towards social media copywriting.

This adventure, without a shadow of a doubt, is constantly evolving and changing, but with very stimulating implications.

6.1 Final remarks

If there is one mantra that is perhaps the most important to follow in order to keep a mind always 'active' while approaching writing, it is that of life-long-learning.

In one' s life, one never stops learning, both from mistakes but also from more transversal experiences which may be far removed from the topic at hand.

That is why it is always good to be open-minded and curious and not to remain vertically 'fixed' on a single field or discipline.

It can sometimes be our passions, our hobbies, travels we have made or something new we have read that stimulate us to give our best and bring new and original proposals.

To inspire, one must be inspired.

6.2 Gratitude

Thank you for devoting your attention to this ebook. And always to you, my best wishes for a peaceful and happy continuation.

Daniele